What We Need?

By Anna White

Scott Foresman
is an imprint of

Glenview, Illinois • Boston, Massachusetts • Chandler, Arizona •
Upper Saddle River, New Jersey

We need a hole.

We need a floor.

We need pipes.

We need walls.

We need a roof.

We need windows.

We need doors.